D0853639

CRICKET SONGS

by the same author

CRICKET SONGS

Japanese haiku
translated by Harry Behn

with pictures selected from
Sesshu and other Japanese masters

HARCOURT, BRACE & WORLD, INC., NEW YORK

© 1964 by Harry Behn
All rights reserved.
Library of Congress Catalog Card Number: 64-11489
Printed in the United States of America

A spark in the sun,
this tiny flower has roots
deep in the cool earth.

HARRY BEHN

It is nice to read
news that our spring rain also
visited your town.

ONITSURA

Over the wintry
forest, winds howl in a rage
with no leaves to blow.

SOSEKI

Asleep in the sun
on the temple's silent bronze
bell, a butterfly...

BUSON

All day in gray rain
hollyhocks follow the sun's
invisible road.

BASHO

A tree frog trilling
softly, the first drop of rain
slips down the new leaves.

ROGETSU

An old silent pond...
A frog jumps into the pond,
   splash! Silence again.

BASHO

Cicadas buzzing
in stillness . . . listen! drilling
in the summer sun. . .

BASHO

Lightning flickering
without sound...how far away
the night-heron cries!

BASHO

Above tides of leaves
that drown the earth, a mountain
stands aloft, alone.

BUSON

Behind me the moon
brushes a shadow of pines
lightly on the floor.

KIKAKU

The red sun sinks low
beyond a dead tree clutching
an old eagle's nest.

BONCHO

The sea hawk hunting
returns to earth as we dance
in smaller circles.

TAIGI

Washing my rice hoe,
ripples flow away...as up
fly the piping snipe!

BUSON

A cloud shimmering
on the still pool . . . a fish stirs
under the water.

SHURIN

A hungry owl hoots
and hides in a wayside shrine . . .
so bright is the moon.

JOSO

Of what use are twigs
but to sweep up a litter
of fallen petals?

BUSON

Beyond the dark trees
lightning flashes on water,
bright, like a vision.

SHIKI

How cool cut hay smells
when carried through the farm gate
as the sun comes up!

BONCHO

An unseen skylark
singing above the mountain
in a mist of sun. . .

SHIKI

Butterfly, these words
from my brush are not flowers,
only their shadows.

SOSEKI

The seed of all song
is the farmer's busy hum
as he plants his rice.

BASHO

My horse clip-clopping
over a field...oh ho! I'm
part of the picture!

BASHO

When spring is gone, none
will so grumpily grumble
as these chirping frogs.

YAYU

A river leaping,
tumbling over rocks roars on...
as the mountain smiles.

MEISETSU

High on a mountain
we heard a skylark singing
faintly, far below.

BASHO

Bent down by a storm,
ripe heads of barley, bowing,
narrow my pathway.

JOSO

Wake up, old sleepy
butterfly! Come, come with me
on my pilgrimage!

BASHO

Above the ruins
of a shrine, a chestnut tree
still lifts its candles.

BASHO

Poor crying cricket,
perhaps your little husband
was caught by our cat.

KIKAKU

Snow fell until dawn.
Now every twig in the grove
glitters in sunlight.

ROKWA

Well! Hello down there,
friend snail! When did you arrive
in such a hurry?

ISSA

One dream all heroes
find to be true...cool green grass
on forgotten tombs.

BASHO

Lightly a new moon
brushes a silver haiku
on the tips of waves.

KYOSHI

Hop out of my way,
Mr. Toad, and allow me
please to plant bamboo!

CHORA

Sun low in the west...
moon floating up in the east...
flowers in shadow...

BUSON

The sea in the dusk
is green, and the sky is green
as a field of rice.

BASHO

We rowed into fog...
and out through fog....Oh how blue,
how bright the wide sea!

SHIKI

This fall of new snow
that sags my hat is my own
and it's light as down.

KIKAKU

A mountain village
deep in snow...under the drifts
a sound of water.

SHIKI

Waiting in darkness,
her smiling face is briefly
lit by a firefly.

ANON

Night over the pond
of the temple garden . . . geese
adrift and asleep. . .

SHIKI

If things were better
for me, flies, I'd invite you
to share my supper.

ISSA

Puffed by a wind, sails
glint on the sea in a quick
bright winter shower.

KYORAI

One man and one fly
buzzing together alone
in a sunny room. . .

ISSA

After the bells hummed
and were silent, flowers chimed
a peal of fragrance.

BASHO

A cautious crow clings
to a bare bough, silently
watching the sunset.

BASHO

Rain went sweeping on
in the twilight, spilling moons
on every grass blade.

SHO-U

What a wonderful
day! No one in the village
doing anything.

SHIKI

Even stones under
mountain waterfalls compose
odes to plum blossoms.

ONITSURA

Out of one wintry
twig, one bud, one blossom's-worth
at last of summer!

RANSETSU

Little bird flitting,
twittering, trying to fly...
my, aren't you busy!

BASHO

At last the sparrows
are fluffing their new feathers
in the sunny dust.

ONITSURA

Evening shadows touch
my gate...high on the mountain
deer still see sun-rays.

BUSON

Turning from watching
the moon, my comfortable old
shadow led me home.

SHIKI

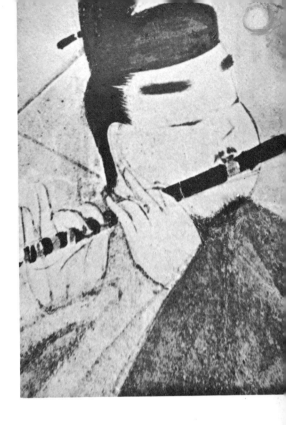

O moon, why must you
inspire my neighbor to chirp
all night on a flute!

KOYO

A baby warbler
gaily swinging upside down
sings his first song.

KIKAKU

Spring is almost gone,
so now this silly old tree
decides to bloom!

BUSON

The tight string broke and
the loose kite fell fluttering,
losing its spirit.

KUBONTA

Since my house burned down,
I now own a better view
of the rising moon.

MASAHIDE

Idly my ship glides,
the tip of its sail dipping
the polished water.

OTSUJI

When my canary
flew away, that was the end
of spring in my house.

SHIKI

Where does he wander
I wonder, my little one
hunting dragonflies?

CHIYO

The least of breezes
blows and the dry sky is filled
with the voice of pines...

ONITSURA

"Day darken!" frogs say
by day. "Bring light, light!" they cry
by night. Old grumblers!

BUSON

Brightly the sun shines
briefly between cloud and sea,
fading as rain falls.

ONTEI

Broken and broken
again on the sea, the moon
so easily mends.

CHOSU

Out of the sky, geese
come honking in the spring's cold
early-morning light.

SOIN

Over the deepest,
darkest river, streams of fire-
flies slowly flowing...

SHIYO

If the white herons
had no voice, they would be lost
in the falling snow.

CHIYO

Swift cloud shadows
darken the maples clinging
by a waterfall.

SHUSEN

Ho, for the May rains
when frogs swim in my open
door for a visit!

SANPU

Tonight in this town
where I was born, my only
friends are the crickets.

ANON

What a pretty kite
the beggar's children fly high
above their hovel!

ISSA

Frog-school competing
with lark-school at dusk softly
in the art of song...

SHIKI

Leaf falling on leaf,
on mounds of leaves, rain splashing
in pools of rain...

GYODAI

I must go begging
for water...morning glories
have captured my well.

CHIYO

In spring the chirping
frogs sing like birds...in summer
they bark like old dogs.

ONITSURA

Whose scarf could this be
but the wind's, thin on the screen
of leaf-gold autumn.

BUSON

That duck, bobbing up
from the green deeps of a pond,
    has seen something strange...

JOSO

Wild ducks have eaten
all my young barley. Alas,
they have flown on.

YASUI

A small hungry child,
told to grind rice, instead
gazes at the moon.

BASHO

O foolish ducklings,
you know my old green pond is
watched by a weasel!

BUSON

Now the moon goes down…
slow through the forest, shadows
drift and disappear.

BUSON

HAIKU

A haiku is a poem in three lines of five, then seven, then five syllables. It is made by speaking of something natural and simple suggesting spring, summer, autumn, or winter. There is no rhyme. Everything mentioned is just what it is, wonderful, here, but still beyond.

> *What a thing to see!*
> *miles and miles of mountains, white*
> *with cherries in bloom . . .*

Sometimes we all make such poems and hardly think about it. The best are as natural as breathing.

THE PICTURES

Except for Sesshu, the artists did not have short, simple names like those the poets made up for themselves. That is why they aren't listed. They wouldn't mind. They were mostly Zen Buddhists and liked to forget themselves.

Farewell! Like a bee
reluctant to leave the deeps
of a peony.

BASHO